Table Of Contents

2

Would You Rather?

Have you ever thought about what type of superhero you'd like to be? What about what food you would like to eat for the rest of your life? What happens if you get stuck in a maze and you need to hop your way out of it? What would you do?

This book is a collection of fun, weird, wacky, and strange questions that puts you into a challenging situation where you have to pick between two choices. This book is great to pull out with your friends and to see how different everyone's answers are.

It's time to choose a category! Get ready to have a laugh, and get ready to have a blast!

How to play

When you and your friends open up this book and start playing, the rules are easy!

1. Each question will give you a choice between two options.

2. Someone will read the options aloud, then everyone has to answer which option they would rather do.

3. No adding other options, it is either one or the other.

4. You can talk about why each person picked their choice, but it isn't needed.

5. The point is to have fun and have a great laugh!

6. There are a lot of questions for hours of fun.

Superpowers & Superheroes

Superheroes are pretty popular, so who wouldn't want to be one or have superpowers? Let's read these questions and see what you think afterward.

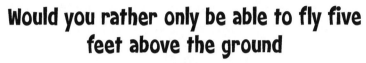

Would you rather only be able to fly five feet above the ground

OR

Be able to fly at any height but only when wearing pink and yellow footie pajamas?

Would you rather be able to talk to sea animals but have to live with them

OR

Be able to stay at home but only be able to talk to rubber ducks in your bathtub?

Would you rather be able to lift an elephant with one hand while your other hand holds an ice cube

OR

Be able to lift buildings but only with your feet?

Would you rather have super hearing for one day a week where you could only hear mice whispering

OR

Have super hearing all the time but only hear fire engine sirens around the world?

Would you rather be able to shoot lasers from your eyes to heat up popcorn

OR

Shoot lasers from your eyes to catch pants on fire when someone is lying?

Would you rather be able to run so fast your toenails never grew

OR

Run so fast that your hair always looks like a flame?

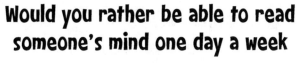

Would you rather be able to read someone's mind one day a week

OR

Hear one person's thoughts for the rest of your life?

Would you rather be able to make fish fly out of a lake to hit someone in the leg

OR

Make fish fly out of the lake and into your frying pan?

Would you rather be invisible only during the day

OR

Be invisible only when it rains?

Would you rather have super strength only in gym class

OR

Have super strength only when you are playing during recess?

Would you rather be able to have super stretchy arms that can only grab pickles

OR

Have super stretchy legs to grow taller but only on the school bus?

Would you rather be able to shrink down to the size of a mouse

OR

Grow bigger than the size of your house?

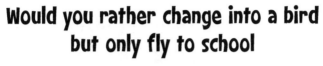

Would you rather change into a bird but only fly to school

OR

Be able to fly anywhere but always have wings?

Would you rather be able to have super smell but only smell stinky feet

OR

Have super smell but only smell stinky cheese?

Would you rather be able to do your homework really fast but only at 3:00 a.m.

OR

Be able to know all the answers to your homework but only for five minutes?

Would you rather know everything for ten seconds a day

OR

Know nothing for one month?

Would you rather be able to super scream but only when giraffes are in trouble

OR

Only be able to super scream for one year?

Would you rather run as fast as a cheetah but only when you have to pee

OR

Fly as fast as a bullet but only when you are late for school?

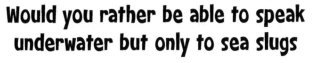

Would you rather be able to speak underwater but only to sea slugs

OR

Be able to speak whales but only when you are in an airplane?

Would you rather be a billionaire supervillain

OR

A struggling superhero who is never paid for doing good?

Would you rather be able to turn into a wolf but only for one minute

OR

Only be able to howl for thirty minutes a day even when someone asks you a question?

Would you rather be able to heat food up with your eyes but can only eat pickles

OR

Heat food up with your eyes but can only eat snails?

Would you rather be able to walk on the sun but only with one leg

OR

Be able to walk on the moon but doing the chicken dance?

Would you rather be able to be in a superhero family but have no powers of your own

OR

Have everyone know you are a superhero and never be able to take the costume off?

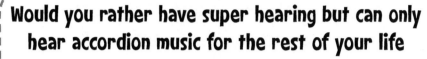

Would you rather have super hearing but can only hear accordion music for the rest of your life

OR

Be able to fly but only to get other people's lunch orders?

Would you rather be able to run really fast but only to school

OR

Have super strength but only be able to lift big bottles of water?

Would you rather be a superhero who could only save super villains

OR

A supervillain whose superpower was only to give evil hugs?

Would you rather run as fast as a car but only to go take a shower

OR

Be able to shoot shower water out of your hand but only to clean mud off of pigs?

Would you rather be rescued by a superhero whose power was to always be on fire

OR

Be a superhero who could only rescue people who were stuck in trees?

Food & Drinks

To keep your body moving and healthy, you have to eat food and drink water every day, but your choices can affect how your body works. Consider that when you are answering the following questions!

Would you rather eat without gaining weight but only eat for twenty minutes a day

OR

Be able to eat throughout the entire day but can only eat oysters?

Would you rather drink soda pop every day for one year but only have one eye open

OR

Drink water for the rest of your life but only use your mouth for breathing?

Would you rather only eat desserts but only at 2:30 a.m.

OR

Only eat tuna sandwiches whenever you are hungry?

Would you rather eat ice cream sundaes with fried grasshoppers on top

OR

Eat a hundred fried grasshoppers covered in chocolate sauce?

Would you rather hunt for your food but you can only eat chicken feet

OR

Have your food caught for you but could eat whatever you could find?

Would you rather eat a steak sandwich covered in worms once a week

OR

Eat a pizza covered in ants once a day?

Would you rather eat your least favorite food once a day

OR

Eat your favorite food but only once every five years?

Would you rather eat ten slices of pizza while riding on the top of a car

OR

Eat ten hot dogs while hiding underneath a car?

Would you rather have someone make you breakfast every day for the rest of your life but only made from the garbage
OR
Make your own breakfast every morning for one week but only stale cereal with seven day-old milk?

Would you rather a waiter bring you the wrong order every time you go out to eat
OR
Do you get the right order every time you eat out but have to pay ten times more than the original price?

Would you rather eat a moldy piece of cheese
OR
Eat 120 pounds of cheese for one meal?

Would you rather wash your mouth with soap
OR
Brush your teeth with frozen peas?

Would you rather eat kangaroo fingers

OR

Eat elephant toes?

Would you rather enjoy a nice meal with your great aunt's skeleton

OR

Eat a terrible meal with your family members?

Would you rather get all the best Halloween candy but can only eat it once a year

OR

Get some not-so-good Halloween candy but watch your brother eat it all?

Would you rather drink lemon juice from a lemon every day

OR

Drink cactus juice from a cactus just once a month?

Would you rather drink the water from a dirty goldfish bowl

OR

Eat the stones from a muddy river?

Would you rather make your own pasta out of flour but can only eat it while sitting on a plane's wing as it flies

OR

Eat cold airplane food for five meals?

Would you rather only be able to microwave your favorite foods

OR

Have to dig your favorite foods out of a grave each time you eat them?

Would you rather have to drink a smoothie with ear wax in it, but you don't know about it

OR

Drink a smoothie with earwax, and you DO know about it?

Would you rather have food only taste like chocolate for the rest of your life

OR

Have food extra spicy one day out of the week?

Would you rather eat ant eggs for one hour each day

OR

Eat frog legs every day and only be able to jump?

Would you rather eat chocolate chip cookies but lose a tooth every time you do

OR

Write down all your secrets and have someone read them to your school?

Would you rather get presents each day for five years that are made of smelly food

OR

Get one present every five years but have it be your favorite food?

Would you rather drink coffee made from mud one day a week for three weeks

OR

Drink a bottle of ketchup, but only one time?

Would you rather drink three bottles of vinegar in one day

OR

Drink a gallon of orange juice every hour for three days?

Would you rather drink the juice of a beetle and see in the dark every time you do

OR

Drink the juice of a star and shine as brightly as one each time?

Would you rather eat underwater with cement shoes once a day

OR

Eat on a galloping horse one time a week?

Would you rather eat an onion like an apple

Or

Eat an apple with a bite already out of it?

Would you rather feed a gorilla a banana with your feet

OR

Wear banana peels on your feet for one week?

Would you rather have ice cubes made out of orange juice in your cola soda

OR

Drink a bowl of clam chowder in the place of water for one week?

Would you rather drink rainwater from a rusty barrel

OR

Use the rust from the barrel as a topping on your ice cream?

Would you rather have donuts for eyes

OR

Like to have hot dogs for feet?

Would you rather find a snake
under your sandwich

OR

Slither like a snake whenever you
eat a sandwich?

Would you rather have a phone made out of
bread that could only call your mom

OR

A conversation with your mom, who is now
made out of bread?

Would you rather drink all your food from a
small baby bottle

OR

Wear visible and big diapers for the rest of
your life?

Would you rather have to walk to a new state to eat your dinner

OR

Drink your water from a pool in your backyard?

Would you rather wear hotdog buns on your feet

OR

Onion rings in your hair?

Sports & Exercise

Do you like to play sports? What about exercise? This category will give you options between some silly situations!

Would you rather play baseball on Mars but only have salmon for shoes

OR

Play baseball with professional players on earth but never catch a ball?

Would you rather be able to dunk a basketball when the basketball hoop is on fire

OR

Hit a baseball with a frozen bat?

Would you rather ride your bicycle blindfolded for exercise

OR

Run in circles for three miles a day?

Would you rather play tag football where the tags are made from fruit roll-ups

OR

Play Marco Polo in the pool where the water is made of jello?

Would you rather kick around a soccer ball but only while walking on your hands

OR

Only be able to talk with a referee's whistle for one full week?

Would you rather walk around in sweaty exercise clothes for a full year without taking a bath

OR

Smell like the sweaty feet of a soccer player for twenty minutes a day for the rest of your life?

Would you rather be able to swim as
fast as an otter but always have otter hair
on your back

OR

Have smooth dolphin skin for three days?

Would you rather be a team mascot who can
dunk a ball but who had to wear a costume
made of honey

OR

Eat all the honey but have a mascot costume
mask for a face for the rest of your life?

Would you rather be able to run like a rabbit
while wearing a turtle shell

OR

Have a turtle shell on except for
when you run?

Would you rather be able to jump like a kangaroo but have its baby in a pouch on your stomach whenever you jump

OR

Stay inside the kangaroo's pouch whenever it was jumping?

Would you rather use a jump rope made out of a boa constrictor

OR

Only be able to jump like a frog every time you ran?

Would you rather use a grapefruit as a basketball for one week

OR

Only be able to dribble spittle from your mouth for two months?

Would you rather ride your bike through the mud for one month with no bath

OR

Ride your bike down a hill and land in a pool of mud?

Would you rather only be able to throw ostrich eggs at your baseball game for one month

OR

Have an ostrich on your team for the entire season?

Would you rather have a chimpanzee on your back when you were playing football

OR

Ride on a chimpanzee's back during a football game?

Would you rather win an Olympic medal for running through spaghetti

OR

Swim through a pool full of toothpicks for a million dollars?

Would you rather set a record for eating octopus tentacles

OR

Be able to squish your body up like a squid to play hide-and-seek better?

Would you rather run like a dog for one year

OR

Gallop like a horse everywhere you went?

Would you rather play hockey with a salami stick instead of a wooden stick

OR

Play hockey with a pizza that your team must eat after the game?

Would you rather be the cheerleader on the top of the pyramid with your hair on fire

OR

Be a cheerleader on the bottom of the pyramid with your hands made out of coins?

Would you rather sail a boat by using your breath

OR

Win a sailing race by pushing one person off the boat every five minutes?

Would you rather do 150 sit ups with the Incredible Hulk sitting on your knees

OR

150 pull-ups with the Incredible Hulk holding onto your legs?

Would you rather have a blowhole on the back of your neck to swim underwater

OR

Gills on the side of your face?

Would you rather play basketball as the shortest person in the room

OR

Play baseball as the slowest person on the team?

Would you rather only be able to scream the score of any sport you are playing for five games

OR

Only scream one time while you are taking a test in class?

Would you rather do jumping jacks while eating macaroni and cheese

OR

Climb a rope with a donut in your mouth but you cannot eat or drop it?

Would you rather watch football for thirty days in a row

OR

Never watch a sport, but automatically know the scores of every game ever played?

Games & Play

Games are a chance to compete with friends and family, and you get to have fun and learn about sportsmanship. But what happens when you have to make some weird choices?

Would you rather be sucked into a video game where an elephant always stepped on you

OR

Be a contestant on a game show where you had ice poured on you every time you answered a question?

Would you rather always win games, but each time you do, your ears grow two sizes

OR

Never win games for the rest of your life?

Would you rather play a game where you got a pie in your face each time you moved your game piece

OR

Have your game piece call you a name any time you move it to the next space?

Would you rather only play hopscotch for the rest of your life

OR

Play any game or activity and always trip over your shoelaces?

Would you rather stuff a hundred pieces of marshmallows in your mouth every day for one month

OR

Stuff a hundred anchovies in your mouth for five minutes?

Would you rather have a computer game that shouted insults at you every time you made a mistake

OR

Play a computer game where you could only make mistakes?

Would you rather have to run on a human-sized hamster wheel for three hours a day to power your phone

OR

Blow into a straw whenever you use your tablet?

Would you rather join a pie-eating contest where the pie crust was made of bug shells

OR

Join a meatball eating contest where the food was made from newspapers?

Would you rather enjoy a board game with a zombie who keeps trying to eat your fingers

OR

A vampire who keeps trying to suck your blood?

Would You Rather For Kids

Would you rather pretend to be a pirate with a parrot that only called you "Shirley"

OR

Pretend to be the parrot with a pirate who only fed you rocks?

Would you rather toss the ball back and forth with your friends but the ball was an eyeball

OR

Toss someone's foot around?

Would you rather turn into a purple teddy bear

Or

A heart-shaped pillow every time you play any sport?

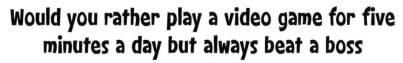

Would you rather play a video game for five minutes a day but always beat a boss

OR

Never beat a boss but get to play for as long as you wanted?

Would you rather play chess where the board pieces were alive and would attack you along with the other pieces

OR

Play on a lifesize board game with other people but only had pillows to fight with?

Would you rather ride a horse who only galloped backward

OR

Wrestle an alligator who sneezed all over you when you touched it?

Would you rather pretend you are a unicorn, but your horn was on your shoulder

OR

Pretend to be a mermaid who had legs and a fish head?

Would you rather be in a dance competition where you could only wear shoes on your hands

OR

Spin around like a top a hundred times?

Would you rather dress up like a puppy for Halloween but always have a tail afterward

OR

Dress as a cat but always have whiskers?

Would you rather climb a tree with a nest of spiders in it

OR

Live in a tree with a nest of birds?

Would you rather have a clown nose stuck to your face for an entire year

OR

Wear only your underpants at school for one day?

Would you rather play with friends for two hours a day but only in the dark

OR

Play with your friends one day a month that has twenty-four hours of light?

Would you rather play a board game with game pieces that bit your fingers

OR

Play a board game that made you walk on nails as a challenge?

Would you rather dance in your room with an audience

OR

Watch an audience dance on TV for the rest of your life?

Would you rather have rainbow clown hair for ten days out of the school year

Or

A bald head for three days?

Would you rather play with action figures who fought back

OR

Be the action figure who always got beat up?

Would you rather be made out of play-doh and only play with yourself

OR

Have only play-doh to play with and a line of people who want to play with you?

Would you rather be in a contest where you knew all the answers but never buzzed first

OR

Burped any time you opened your mouth to answer the questions?

Weird & Wacky

Wherever real or imagined, having the choice to make between weird and wacky sure is a lot of fun!

Would You Rather For Kids

Would you rather have one big eye in the middle of your forehead

OR

Have two small noses on your face?

Would you rather roller skate with a giraffe

OR

Dance with a crocodile?

Would you rather wear snakes from your ears

OR

Caterpillars on your eyebrows?

Would you rather have a blue and white striped tongue

OR

Skin that turned purple in the sunlight?

Would you rather have to eat ice cubes made with toilet water every day

OR

Eat just one piece of a mud sandwich?

Would you rather only be able to travel by pogo stick

OR

Only be able to travel by riding a turtle?

Would You Rather For Kids

Would you rather be able to hop on one foot for two weeks

OR

Walk on your hands for three hours?

Would you rather get shot out of a cannon into a pile of whoopie cushions

OR

Get shot out of a cannon and land on a pile of cushions that smelled like tuna?

Would you rather have chewing gum that smelled like a lunchroom

OR

Pop balloons that smelled of rotten eggs?

Would you rather blow bubbles from your mouth every time you speak

OR

Fart bubbles when you were trying to walk to school?

Would you rather have an extra finger that is very long

OR

An extra toe that is always visible from your shoes?

Would you rather eat ice cream that was made from fish

OR

Eat fish that screamed each time you bit into it?

Would you rather walk like a chicken
for one month

OR

Dance like a toddler for the rest of your life?

Would you rather be a bumblebee with
no stinger

OR

Be a human with a stinger for a nose?

Would you rather have blue polka dots on
your face for three months

OR

Only be able to burp when you spoke?

Would you rather watch a baby's TV show for the rest of your life

OR

Only be able to sleep on Sundays?

Would you rather be able to only walk on water (never swim or bathe)

OR

Only swim and bathe in pickle juice?

Would you rather wear glasses so you could only see ghosts

OR

Be a ghost who only haunted funhouses?

Would you rather have a cat who told the answers to tests, but they were all wrong

OR

Have a hamster who told your secrets to your friends but gave you the right test answers?

Would you rather only be able to walk on the ceiling for one month

OR

Only be able to crawl on the ground for twenty minutes each day?

Would you rather watch someone's nose grow to poke you in the eye

OR

Have someone poke you in the eye every day for one month?

Would you rather learn how to karate chop a salmon

OR

Hammer a hotdog into a wall like a nail?

Would you rather make everyone laugh all the time

OR

Make only one person laugh once a day?

Would you rather only be able to watch horror movies

OR

Watch anything but be blindfolded so you could only hear the shows?

Would you rather always have goosebumps
OR
Always be sweating?

Would you rather constantly itch your nose
OR
Always have a cough?

Would you rather only wear one pair of pants
for the rest of your life
OR
Only be able to wear mismatched socks?

Would you rather only be able to quack like a duck when you were angry

OR

Be mad all the time but only speak in French?

Would you rather wear clothing made out of fallen leaves for three days

OR

Eat a pile of leaves in one sitting?

Would you rather have an almond in place of one of your eyes

OR

Have a pine cone for a nose?

Would you rather live in an life-sized fish bowl by yourself

OR

Live on an ice cream truck with five other people?

Would you rather be able to understand what a cat was saying during the full moon

OR

Only be able to speak like a cat any time you had to answer a question?

Would you rather live in a circle made out of cheesecake

OR

Live in a square that had spaghetti carpeting?

Would you rather stretch your body out ten minutes a day

OR

Have your arms and legs made out of rubber for six months?

Would you rather live on a cloud where it only rained rocks

OR

Live on a rock where it only rained pork chops?

Would you rather live in a forest made of rubber

OR

Live in a house made of glass?

Would You Rather For Kids

Would you rather only be able to start fires with your breath

OR

Smell like fire for the rest of your life?

Would you rather be full bald

OR

Covered from head to leg with dense hair?

Would you rather only wear a bunny-rabbit costume for three months in a row

OR

Wear footie pajamas to school for one day a week for three weeks?

Would you rather have a pet that is part bird, part lizard, and only ate blue cheese

OR

Have a pet made of blue cheese that only eats one time a year?

Would you rather use a public toilet that is too dirty

OR

Will use one that is dark and has a snake in it?

Gross or Grosser

This section is NOT for the faint of heart. Which choice is the grossest one? Only you can decide.

Would you rather have a finger stuck up your nose for thirty days

OR

Smell like poop for one day?

Would you rather be a potato who ate French fries

OR

The potato who turns into the French fries?

Would you rather have to eat a live rat who calls you "John"

OR

Pick something from your teeth using a rusty nail?

Would you rather eat moldy cheese that sat in the sun for ten days

OR

Wear moldy cheese to school for five days?

Would you rather make funny sounds whole day long

OR

Have a tree growing over your head?

Would you rather bleed from your nose every day for twenty minutes

OR

Bleed from your eyes for one week a year?

Would you rather have to eat a raccoon that was hit by a car

OR

Eat one day a month but only from the garbage can?

Would you rather walk through sewer water every day to get to school

OR

Smell like sewer water one day a month?

Would you rather that your hair be made out of boogers

OR

That your breath always smells like cat food?

Would you rather always have a pimple on your nose that talked during class

OR

Have a pimple pop all over the other students in your class?

Would you rather pee your pants every time you watched a scary movie

OR

Live in pee pants for a month?

Would you rather have to keep your toes in your mouth for one year

OR

Keep your fingers in your ears once a day for five years?

Would you rather vomit every day
for one year

OR

Watch someone else vomit for
twelve hours?

Would you rather walk barefoot over a
road of slugs

OR

Eat live, raw slugs for breakfast every
day for one week?

Would you rather eat raw eggs while the
chicken who laid them watches

OR

Eat raw chicken in front of other chickens?

Would you rather wash your hair mud

OR

Brush your teeth with garlic?

Would you rather dance in a pile of mashed potatoes

OR

Only eat mashed potatoes for one year?

Would you rather have a pet that was made only out of slime and sneezed all over your friends

OR

Sneeze on your friend each time someone says your name?

Would You Rather For Kids

Would you rather eat a bowl full of bugs

OR

Lick the undersides of fifty rocks that have sat in cow poop?

Would you rather learn how to play piano with your toes

OR

Only be able to drink milk through a straw in your nose?

Would you rather drink the water from your goldfish's bowl

OR

Eat the algae out of a goldfish pond?

Would you rather clean your grandma's toes out

OR

Wash your dog's bum?

Would you rather only hear a cowbell ring anytime anyone said your name

OR

Have to fling cow poo at someone instead of saying their name?

Would you rather eat a handful of wet dog food

OR

Eat a handful of dried ants eggs?

Would you rather roll in a pile of dirty money to take a bath

OR

Not be able to take a bath for two months?

Would you rather have an itch in your pants that doesn't go away for two weeks

OR

An itch in your nose that happens one time a day, every day, for five years?

Would you rather have to watch your parents kiss and hug for two days

OR

Watch your little brother pick his nose for two hours?

Would you rather run through raining dog poo

OR

Walk through a storm of dinosaur vomit?

Would you rather have to dissect an animal in biology class

OR

Eat a raw piece of frog's legs?

Would you rather suck a worm through a straw

OR

Have a snail slime you when you are sleeping?

Would you rather slather toe jam on a piece of bread and give it to someone for breakfast

OR

Have to clean out the ear wax from a toothbrush?

Would you rather see something that made you gag for thirty minutes a day

OR

Throw up once a day every two weeks for one month?

Would you rather find mold growing in your belly button

OR

Find mold growing in your bed?

Would you rather see bugs crawling on your favorite toy

OR

Be a life-sized bug that crawls all over everyone else's stuff?

Would you rather eat a fuzzy ball of cotton

OR

Have cotton mouth for six days?

Would you rather learn how to make ice cream made out of slime

OR

Have to wash your feet in slime for two months?

Your Body or Your Mind

What is going on with your body? What happens if something goes wonky? Which scenario would you rather have more?

Would you rather be able to read a thousand books in two weeks

OR

Walk a thousand miles in thirty days?

Would you rather be able to learn all the dances in the world in one day

OR

Be able to learn all the languages?

Would you rather discover a new soft-shelled crab

OR

Climb a rocky mountain in record time?

Would you rather be the fastest sledding champion ever

OR

Be able to repeat an entire dictionary back to another person?

Would you rather have a memory, where you can only remember the color of someone's nose hair

OR

Have nose hair so long you can braid it?

Would you rather read something you enjoy but never be able to sit down

OR

Only be able to sit down without reading anything good?

Would you rather learn a how to cook a new recipe every day, but you only learned recipes with flowers in them

OR

Cook a soup made from monkey's brains one time a year?

Would you rather have fingers that were long like an alien's limbs

OR

Legs that wobble like you are walking on piles of jello?

Would you rather enjoy the sounds surround you, even if they are a jack hammer

OR

Hate the sounds around you, even if it is a babbling brooke?

Would You Rather For Kids

Would you rather see like a rabbit

OR

Jump like a frog?

Would you rather have a septum-ring in your nose all the time

OR

Wear the horns of a bull for three weeks?

Would you rather be able to read all the books, but only if they were in MEOW

OR

Read all the books but not be able to explain them except in MEOW?

Would you rather be able to calculate any math problem in your head

OR

Be able to know the answer to any question before it is even asked?

Would you rather memorize any book you read but only if you read it at night

OR

Only be able to read during the day, but it can only be one book?

Would you rather have a tail growing out of your bum

OR

Have a horn growing out of your head?

Would You Rather For Kids

Would you rather have three eyes

OR

Have four arms?

Would you rather be able to crawl like a spider but live on a web

OR

Be able to slither like a snake and live in a hole?

Would you rather have two of your legs be dog legs

OR

Have two arms of a T-Rex?

Would you rather have a chance to win a million dollars by knowing everything

OR

A chance to win a million cookies but not know anything?

Would you rather be able to read any book in existence but only read it backward

OR

Be able to climb any mountain in the world but have to do it by hopping like a kangaroo?

Would you rather be able to do a hundred chin-ups in the gym but only because you have tentacles for fingers

OR

Have the beak of a bird that can help you eat nuts?

Would you rather be able to drop a box of coins on the floor and be able to count them but always get the number wrong

OR

Count all the coins right but have a fear of money?

Would you rather think about things in colors and sound, but only have the sound be a car horn and the color be hot pink

OR

Think about things in smell and sight, but only smell pickles and see lamas?

Would you rather be afraid of feathers

OR

Have feathers grown out of your head?

Would you rather be soft like a rabbit

OR

Silky like a snake?

Would you rather have goldfish eyes transplanted in the side of your head

OR

Have a third arm transplanted on the back of your neck?

Space or Pirates

If you had a choice between pirates or astronauts, what would you choose? The ocean and space hold such vast unknowns, so only our imaginations can answer the following crazy questions!

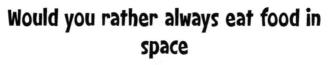
Would you rather always eat food in space

OR

Only be able to go to the bathroom in space?

Would you rather float on the sea

OR

Float in a spaceship?

Would you rather have no gravity every time you showered

OR

Could only shower with ocean water?

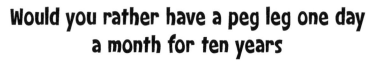

Would you rather have a peg leg one day a month for ten years

OR

Have to wear an astronaut's helmet for one hour a day for one year?

Would you rather take a dog who can speak alien to space with you

OR

A monkey who can speak pirate on a boat with you?

Would you rather find moon rocks

OR

Search for buried treasure?

Would you rather dress as an astronaut on a pirate ship

OR

Dress like a pirate on a spaceship?

Would you rather meet a ghost on a haunted pirate ship

OR

Meet an alien from a new planet?

Would you rather learn more about how whales talk to pirates

OR

Figure out how to work a toilet in space?

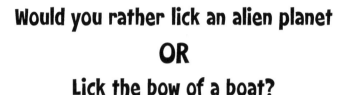

Would you rather lick an alien planet

OR

Lick the bow of a boat?

Would you rather fix the outside of a spaceship and only be connected by a small hose

OR

Scrape off all the barnacles off a ship by using your fingers and nails?

Would you rather dance with a martian

OR

Swim with a mermaid?

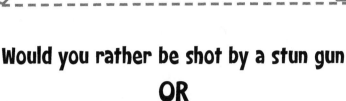

Would you rather be shot by a stun gun
OR
Pushed off the plank of a pirate ship?

Would you rather be a pirate captain
OR
The astronaut who makes the food?

Would you rather float alone in space for thirty minutes
OR
Float alone in the sea for one week?

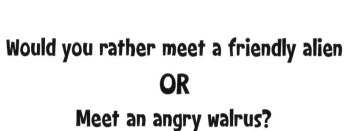

Would you rather meet a friendly alien

OR

Meet an angry walrus?

Would you rather swim with the turtles

OR

Fly past the sun?

Would you rather time travel back to when your parents were your age

OR

Spend a decade with a real pirate crew?

Would you rather only eat lemons limes, and oranges

OR

Eat dehydrated meatloaf?

Would you rather play leapfrog with a space alien

OR

Play tag with a crocodile?

Would you rather be trapped on a deserted island with your parrot

OR

Be stuck on a deserted planet by yourself?

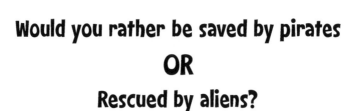

Would you rather be saved by pirates
OR
Rescued by aliens?

Would you rather have an eye patch
OR
Have a peg leg?

Would you rather have a mustache that always catches on fire
OR
Have five teeth missing?

Would you rather sleep standing up
OR
Sleep in three feet of water?

Would you rather be friends with the mice on the boats
OR
Talk to the space rocks you collect?

Would you rather live on a spaceship with an alien family
OR
Have an alien family live with you in your bedroom?

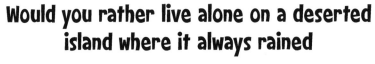

Would you rather live alone on a deserted island where it always rained

OR

Live on a pirate ship with only crabs for your crew?

Next Read

Don't miss the second book of this series...

Would Your Rather Book For Kids

300+ Hilarious, Silly, and Challenging Questions To Make You Laugh

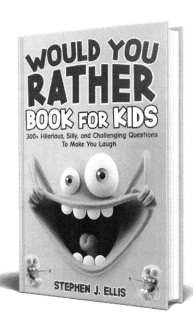

Go To The Below URL:

www.thestephenellis.com/wur1

Want More Books By Stephen Ellis?

Go To The Below URL:

www.thestephenellis.com/books

Made in the USA
Columbia, SC
08 August 2024

07b1a71e-81e2-4899-9a95-d862b5a916baR01